Big Machines At Work

Graders

By Hal Rogers

The Child's World® Inc. ◆ Eden Prairie, Minnesota

Published by The Child's World®, Inc.
7081 W. 192 Ave.
Eden Prairie, MN 55346

Design and Production:
The Creative Spark, San Juan Capistrano, CA

Photos: © 1998 David M. Budd Photography

Library of Congress Cataloging-in-Publication Data

Rogers, Hal.
     Graders / by Hal Rogers.
        p. cm.
     Summary: Describes the parts of a grader, how it works, and the work it does
at a construction site.
     ISBN 1-56766-653-1 (lib. bdg. : alk. paper)
     1. Graders (Earthmoving machinery) Juvenile literature. [1. Graders (Earthmoving
machinery)] I. Title.
TA725.R633 1999
624.1'52—dc21
                                                             99-20858
                                                               CIP

Contents

On the Job

On the job, graders work at a **construction site.** A grader makes the ground flat. The ground must be flat before workers put up a building.

A grader uses a long metal **blade.**

The blade scrapes away dirt.

There is a **computer** at the construction site. It can tell when the ground is flat. Then the grader can move to another part of the site.

Workers also use graders to build

smooth roads.

A grader can travel across rough ground.

It has special wheels.

The driver can move the wheels up and down.

Some graders have sharp **ripper teeth.**

They loosen up rocks and hard dirt.

A grader moves too slowly to go to

the gas station.

A truck brings fuel to the construction site.

Workers fill up the tank.

17

Climb Aboard!

Would you like to see where the driver sits?

A grader's driver is called an **operator.**

He sits in the **cab.** He uses special **levers** to

make the grader work. He steers the grader

with a steering wheel.

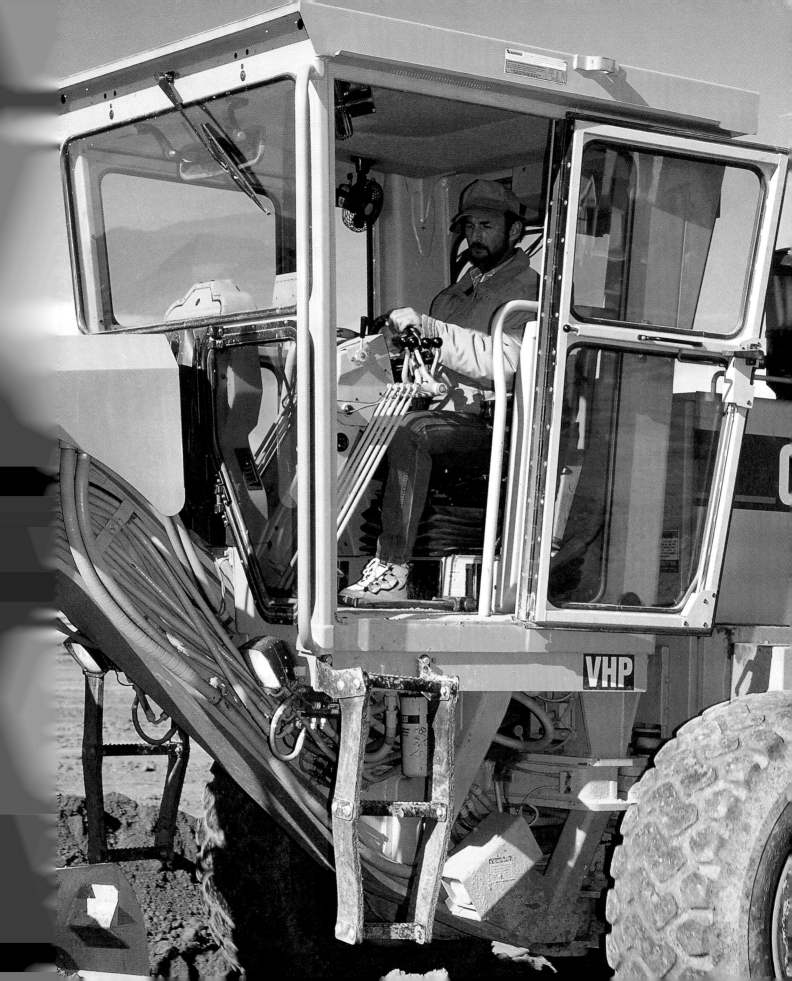

Up Close

The inside

1. The operator's seat

2. The levers

3. The steering wheel

21

The outside

1. The blade

2. The ripper teeth

3. The cab

4. The wheels

Glossary

blade (BLAYD)
The blade is a long piece of metal on a grader. It scoops up dirt like a shovel.

cab (KAB)
A cab is the place where the grader's driver sits. It has a seat, a steering wheel, and levers.

computer (kum-PYOOT-ur)
A computer is a machine that can figure information. Some construction sites have a computer that can tell when the land is flat.

construction site (kun-STRUCK-shun SITE)
A construction site is a place where workers build something. Workers make buildings at a construction site.

levers (LEV-erz)
The grader's levers are metal bars with black knobs at the end. The operator uses them to move the machine.

operator (OPP-er-ay-ter)
The operator is the person who drives the grader. He or she also makes the machine work.

ripper teeth (RIP-per TEETH)
The ripper teeth are pieces of sharp metal on the back of a grader. The ripper teeth loosen rocks and hard dirt.